ORGANISE YOUR HOME OFFICE

Become
dynamic and effective

Dr Sandy Clyne

Organise Your Home Office

Copyright © 2011, Dr Sandy Clyne

ISBN: 978-1-4457-6791-8

Second edition: August 2011

All Rights Reserved. No part of this publication may be reproduced, stored in a retrieval system, or transmitted, in any form or by any means, electronic or mechanical, through the use of photocopying, recording or otherwise, without prior written permission from the author.

This book is sold subject to the condition that it shall not, by way of trade or otherwise, be lent, resold, hired out or otherwise circulated without the author's prior written consent, in any form of binding or cover other than that in which it is published, and without a similar condition including this condition, being imposed on the subsequent purchaser.

Organise your home office

Acknowledgements

Enormous thanks to everyone who helped me along the rocky road to publication, particularly:

The home office users who

- drew my attention to their difficulties,
- inspired me to write this book,
- spurred me into finding better ways to run a home office.

Colleagues, clients, and friends who

- encouraged and supported me through difficulties,
- challenged my suggestions,
- provided stimulating ideas.

My family, particularly:

- husband Kenn, whose support and patience helped me through technical and creative crises,
- the 'girls', my daughters Suzanne and Nina, whose support and belief in me never fails.

The team who guided me through the final stages of book production:

- Lisa Rossetti, coach extraordinaire,
- Diane Stafford, whose web design and wicked sense of humour cheered and inspired me,
- editor/designer Viv, for her encouragement and cunning suggestions,
- Judith and Albert, the cartoonists, who each expressed so vividly the world of the home office user.

Contents

Foreword	**9**
Introduction	**10**
Who has a home office?	10
Background to the modern office	15
Who needs this book?	19
How to use this book	21
Why am I so disorganised?	**25**
Self-assessment	**29**
The story of your disorganisation	30
Questionnaire: Recognise your difficulties	33
Your work style personality	39
What else affects my ability to be organised?	**45**
Task overload	45
Interruptions and distractions	46
Procrastination	46
Beliefs	47
Bad habits	48
A final thought	49
How to be more organised	**51**
Why do you want to be organised?	**55**
Seven steps to an organised you	**57**
Step One: Find your purpose	57
Step Two: Create your vision of the future	59
Step Three: Your excuses for being disorganised	60
Step Four: Set your organising goals	63
Step Five: Methods for becoming organised	65
Step Six: Support	79
Step Seven: The future	81

Sorting out your office problems — 83
Arranging your office: the basics — 85
Working in your office — 87
    Combining work and home — 89
    Home-based disturbances — 91
    Creating your personal home office space — 92
    Reducing procrastination — 93
    Getting tasks done — 96
Delegating — 97
Reading and writing — 101
    Tips for more effective reading — 102
    Tips for more effective writing — 104
    Tips for editing — 106
    Tips for improving your memory — 107
Paperwork mountain — 109
    Information management — 113
    Current projects — 117
    Reference files — 118
    Pruning your files — 120
    Electronic filing — 121
    Paperless office — 122
    Keep in touch – even when you're out — 122

Future action — 125
Your action plan — 128
Maintaining a clear vision — 131

Examples and resources — 133
Snapshots of home office life — 135
Resources — 147

Organise your home office

Foreword

Through the effects of brain damage from a head injury, I lost my ability to organise ANYTHING. This, of course, affected every part of my life, but was especially important in my work as a freelance business psychologist, because the home office was the centre of my professional life.

The effects of the accident turned my office into a nightmare of chaos and disorganisation. As I recovered, I created, or perhaps recreated, ways to be organised, so I could carry on with my work.

Eventually, I began to understand that I wasn't unique in having problems with an untidy home office. The increasing spread of the home office as the most common place to work, has led to the world becoming full of hidden away offices in a constant muddle.

The home office is not only the office of the future but of the present. As it is a new way of working, there are new problems. Yet people are generally being left to find their own way of organising in this new context.

Whoever you are, whatever your focus, if you ever use part of your home as an office, this book has been written for you.

Introduction

WHO HAS A HOME OFFICE?

Since the personal computer became commonplace, the answer is, quite simply, all kinds of people - and the numbers are growing all the time.

It has been estimated that there are over five million people in the UK who work in this way, and the development of technology continues to reduce the need for everyone to have fixed working locations and rigid working hours.

The personal computer has changed everything. Today, few students would dream of submitting a project hand-written. Hardly any club committee members work without a computer to keep track of paperwork or team changes.

Furthermore, every small business depends on computers to manage every aspect of their work. Office work has changed dramatically over recent decades, mainly because of new technology, together with improved communications. These have also led to social changes, such as women starting many entrepreneurial mum-at-home businesses, supported by the essential computer and home office.

Forget the traditional 9-5 full-time pattern of office working. Flexibility, powered by the home computer is now the name of the game.

People who have a working office at home include:

- part-time workers - such as women, who arrange their schedules to fit around domestic commitments.

- those who work flexi-time, with some core time and time off for other activities, which can include some work in the home office.

- job-sharers - common for professionals such as teachers, lawyers, nurses.

- home-based workers - i.e. those who have their own business or work part-time from home.

- free-lance professionals and contractors working from home.

- those who work a variable year – particularly jobs with fluctuating quiet and busy periods, such as accountancy or book-keeping.

- people who work in several different places - e.g. in the office, abroad, and at home.

- staff who do a lot of travelling, such as reps and consultants, who can now keep in touch via laptops, mobiles, and email.

- those who work outside the traditional 9-5 hours. Working different hours of the day, across the globe, means that unsocial hours are common.

- charity/voluntary group/committee workers.

- students at school/college/university.

Of course, all those on the list above have a different focus and purpose, but what do they have in common?

The answer is:

> The need to organise all the activities of an office, plus the added difficulty of
>
> - working in a place which is also their home and
>
> - being without standard office services, such as a technician to fix the computer, or the post-room for post and parcels.

Working in this way has both advantages and disadvantages, which include:

Advantages

- Control over your schedule.

- Nobody keeping an eye on you.

- Freedom from workplace distractions.

- The opportunity to combine personal and leisure activities around work, instead of limiting them to inflexible hours outside work-time.

- Taking a holiday or going on a course, whenever convenient.

- Increase in the choices and flexibility you have in your working day.

- Childcare arrangements are simpler.

- You have the best of both worlds, balancing work and personal life.

- No commuting time.

- You can respond positively to emergencies and new opportunities.

Disadvantages

- Absence of boundaries between work and home life can mean that you're paying the milkman instead of writing that million-pound proposal.

- Your work area may spill over into home space, particularly if you have children. It's sometimes difficult to maintain physical boundaries, even if they've been formally agreed, as the reality of home life means that you don't have total control over other family members' activities.

- You find that you have to be the entire office support system: Not only do you make your own coffee, but you also have to fix the computer, post the letters, order stationery and do your own filing.

- You may miss having colleagues, even if you've previously found them difficult. Lack of human contact and stimulation can make you feel very isolated.

- Your workspace may be limited, as you may not be allowed to use all the rooms you would like: *"Do you think this is all your office, dear? It's still our house, you know!"*

- If you're starting a new business from the box room or a craft business from the cellar, you will find that you have to plan all the equipment and furnishings, buy them and also clean up each day after you finish work.

- Unless you go out, there may be no-one over the age of six to talk to.

BACKGROUND TO THE MODERN OFFICE

The office as we know it today was created in the 19th Century, to deal with all aspects of the new worlds of finance, industry, business and commerce.

Until the introduction of the PC, which led to the home office, there was a clear role in the office for everybody, from the Managing Director to the office boy. Today, in the home office - particularly for a business - anyone can take on any role, from CEO to secretary, post-girl, cleaner, technician or all of these at once.

In addition, there is now the additional spicy ingredient of the family nearby, or even intruding into, the office. This can add a great deal of bite to the mix.

Because the home office is often used by many family members, it becomes, in effect, the family office. This can bring new problems, played out through games such as *"Where are my files?"* and, *"Who's used my password?"* which can lead to areas of family conflict and disagreement - computer envy can be a major source of discord and may even become part of family therapy.

Organising your home office doesn't sound very sexy or exciting. Although ordering the right size envelopes, writing a client report or an essay for your tutor may not be the cutting-edge of technology, it nevertheless helps you to achieve what you want, which is being effective at what you do. This provides job satisfaction for you, and appreciation from clients and co-workers.

Organise your home office

Introduction

Organising effectively isn't a glamorous or appealing activity, but . . .

it helps you to achieve what you want easily, and makes important tasks simple to manage.

Organise your home office

Introduction

WHO NEEDS THIS BOOK?

Ask yourself, are you:

- drowning under a deluge of emails?
- buried beneath a barrage of paper?
- secretly addicted to procrastinating?
- uncertain about your priorities?
- irritated by how your office looks?
- struggling to read fast enough to cope with all the paperwork?
- wishing your writing could be improved?
- unclear about your objectives?
- planning projects badly?

Did you answer "**YES**" to any of these questions? Then read on…

You need this book if:

- you use a computer and a home office for personal, professional, educational, or business-related purposes.

- You're fed-up with being bogged-down with the day-to-day running of the office.

- your disorganisation is confusing you and affecting your energy and effectiveness.

- you want to reduce office chaos and create a place that works easily and simply.

- You're sure that there are ways to have a home office that's a heaven instead of a hell, if you only knew how.

The **objective** of this book is to make you more effective at running your home-based office, however big or small, whatever its purpose: whether it's in a corner of the kitchen, the spare bedroom, shed in the garden, or the latest hi-tech luxury haven.

The useful tips and methods described in this book will allow you to shift your energy and focus, away from struggling with the activities of office management, towards doing more of what you want to do - the work itself.

You will move from being a harassed and overloaded juggler of priorities to becoming a more focused, organised, and calm professional.

HOW TO USE THIS BOOK

The book is divided into five sections:

1. **Why am I so disorganised?** Understanding why you tackle office work the way you do currently.

2. **How to be more organised:** Changing your beliefs and habits, so you can function better.

3. **Sorting out your office problems:** Details of how to cope with common problems associated with organising.

4. **Future action plan:** How to stay organised.

5. **Example case studies and Resources:** Case studies and useful support materials.

Before you begin to study this book, start a notebook/workbook of your own, to record any notes, comments, observations and ideas.

> Choose a note-book which is visually pleasing and has a format which suits the way you work:
>
> - e.g. with blank pages, so that you can draw diagrams and illustrations as well as make notes
>
> or with . . .
>
> - wide margins?
> - narrow lines?
> - coloured dividers to separate the sections?

This workbook will become a record of your journey from chaos to order.

Next, look at the Contents page and note any sections that interest you. List them in your notebook, including details such as page numbers or section names, so you can find them again. Mark the book itself with highlighters, post-it notes and/or notes in the margin. This will help you to find key sections when you suddenly realise you've found something important to you.

Don't try to keep either your note-book or this book pristine and tidy - on the contrary, your jottings are a record of your journey through the dark world of disorganisation.

Your workbook and this book are working documents through which you will be able to create your organised office.

First, quickly scan this book from cover to cover. This will give you an impression and general overview from which you can begin to plan your campaign to transform yourself from '**Disorganised Me**' into a completely new creature: '**Organised Me**'.

This book is your first step towards becoming more organised; it will not cure you, but will provide a framework to which you can refer whenever you need to work out your next step and check your progress.

Your involvement and commitment, together with this book, will help you to make the changes you need. It's an active partnership, to make you more organised and successful.

Organise your home office

Part 1

Why am I so Disorganised?

Pandemonium!

Organise your home office

Why am I so disorganised?

Before you begin your '*Reorganise Me*' project, the first thing you need to know is more about **how** and **why** you're disorganised. You need to look at the reasons in all their awfulness, as this is the first step towards becoming more focused.

What do you want to get out of this book? Are you reading it because:

a)   it might be interesting or relevant to your life, but it's not a high priority? or...

b)   you know that being more organised will make a huge difference to the quality, success and satisfaction of what you do?

If the answer is a)
Look at the Contents page and ask yourself: "*Could any of this improve how I work in my office?*" If the response is, "*Yes, of course*", then use the book to examine and remedy your difficulties.

If the answer is b)
You've already realised that an important question for your office is: "*How can I be more organised?*"

In either case, using this book can make all the difference to your success, and transform how organised you are and what you can achieve. You need to look at your disorganisation in more detail.

Particularly:

1. what you do in your home office right now.
2. how you would like your office to be in the future.

This is the **first step** in your transformation from "*Well, I suppose it'll do*" to "*I know I could do it better*" and finally "*I've done a really good job and I enjoyed doing it*".

Living with disorganisation, but not being aware of its effect on what you do, constantly stops you from achieving as much as you could.

You already have some idea of your particular areas of difficulty, so carrying out a detailed self-assessment won't be pleasant, but this activity lets you see your problems in more detail, revealing any destructive patterns and bad habits.

In the **first** half of this section, you will use self-assessment to reveal more about how and why you're disorganised.

The **second** half of the section will explain in more detail how internal and external influences have caused your organising problems and can also contribute to improvements in your ability to be organised.

Are you ready to face yourself? If so, here we go.

Self-assessment

Your self-assessment has three parts:

1. The story of your disorganisation.

2. A questionnaire which will show your weaknesses in particular areas of organising.

3. Recognising your work style personality.

Together, these will show the particular aspects of your behaviour that you need to modify, so that you can match them to the activities and advice in later sections.

From these, you can learn new organising skills and then create a way of continuing to practise these new skills, without slipping back into old bad habits.

THE STORY OF YOUR DISORGANISATION

In your workbook, write a letter to yourself describing how you work now. You might think you don't really know, but really you do, and this exercise will bring the details into your conscious awareness.

Imagine you're a good friend to yourself — someone who has your best interests at heart but will be truthful with you.

Here's the beginning:

> 'Dear (your name here),
>
> 'I want to be better at organising myself in my home office. I want to:
>
> - Do less of X (list items),
>
> - Be better at Y (list items),
>
> - And also Z (list anything else you want to add to what's above).'

Write your letter in an informal and friendly way as if it's from someone who knows you well and really tells it how it is.

From this letter, you will see:

> - What gives you the most trouble, and what you would like to change, improve or do differently.
>
> - What you do well and would like to do more of.
>
> - New things you would like to do in the future.

Summarise the items above, in your notebook. This will give you a clearer idea of what you do badly, but also what you do well and want to continue and improve. This letter essentially lays out what you already unconsciously knew - but there's a power in seeing it written down, which can lead to action and results.

Improvement comes from

- knowledge of what doesn't work now,

- a vision of what would work better,

- which then becomes a plan to implement.

Do you have any particular quality or habit which can sometimes be unhelpful but at other times useful?

An example of how a particular pattern of behaviour can be both good and bad for you is Amy's story:

One of her major strengths was perseverance: she stuck to her plans doggedly until they were complete, and so finished everything on time (no procrastination for Amy). However, the downside was that she also stuck with committees and projects which were going nowhere, as she considered that having made a commitment, she had to stick with it whatever happened.

This pattern of behaviour led her into many dead-ends. Her perseverance only worked when she was clear about her objectives for the project and could see distractions that were taking her in another direction and so was able to avoid them.

Organise your home office

In contrast, Donna started many new things with enthusiasm, but this fizzled away when faced with long-term action. As a child, she had never finished her piano lessons and at work, she was known for being erratic and unreliable. Because she wasn't seen as being consistent, she missed out on anything that needed long-term commitment.

Think about recent work you've done. Do you find that you repeat the same unsuccessful patterns of behaviour over and over again? If so, you need to catch yourself and STOP falling into the same trap. Don't let yourself become bogged down by bad habits.

QUESTIONNAIRE: RECOGNISE YOUR DIFFICULTIES

We all have a particular '*organising personality*'. Discovering yours will give you another way to find out how to become more organised.

Note: There are no right or wrong answers to the questions below, as the purpose of the questionnaire is to show you what you need to focus on, to become better organised - your YES answers show what you need to concentrate on improving.

This exercise builds on what you saw in the letter to yourself. Together, these provide a template for what you need to work on.

Answer each question as honestly as you can.

1. **What do you do with any unnecessary items of mail, e.g. post or emails?**

    a) ignore them?
    b) bin them?
    c) add them to the "*Don't know what to do with it*" pile?
    d) pass them on?

2. **Do you have to read magazines and journals as part of your work, e.g. to keep up to date? What do you do with them...?**

    a) File them/cut out the relevant bits, and file those, throwing away the rest of the magazine?
    b) Pile them up
    c) Pass them on

3. **When reading, do you:**

    a) read fast enough?
    b) know your reading speed?

c) want to read faster / better?
d) prefer screen to books?
e) prefer books to screen?

4. **When you write (an email/ memo/ report/ letter), do you write it on screen or by hand?**

   a) on screen
   b) by hand

5. **How do you prevent yourself from being interrupted during your working day?**

   a) Switch off the phone?
   b) Have a regular period (e.g. Friday afternoon, or 08:30–09:00 in the morning) when you signal "*Do not interrupt*".
   c) Love interruptions (and even create your own).

6. **What is usually your understanding of the documents you read?**

   a) Perfect.
   b) Could be better.
   c) Some documents make no sense - do you think this is a failing of yours?

7. **How is your memory?**

   a) Not so good for some things.
   b) I know which parts of my memory need improvement.

8. **Do you knowingly procrastinate?**

   a) I put off doing urgent things which should be done immediately, or at least very soon.
   b) I procrastinate when panicking over a pile-up of unmet deadlines.

9. **How are your focus and concentration?**

   a) I'm easily distracted.
   b) I keep focused all the time, no matter what happens.

10. **Meetings:**

   a) I'm well prepared.
   b) I follow-up on action points.
   c) I often find myself in meetings where I'm unsure why I'm there.
   d) My preparation is sketchy and I forget to follow-up any points.

11. **Are your files (paper and computer)**

   a) a complete mess?
   b) thoroughly organised?
   c) you keep meaning to sort them out?

12. **Are your documents well prepared? Are you**

   a) careful about editing and presenting?
   b) a bit slap-dash and couldn't care less, or even say "*it'll do*".

13. **Delegation handled?**

   a) I know what others can do instead of me.
   b) I hang on to all jobs ("*they wouldn't understand how to do it properly*").

14. **How well do you use time?**

   a) I'm a planner, with every minute worked out in advance - each day/week/month/year is arranged beforehand.
   b) I'm a bumbler, lurching from crisis to crisis, fire-fighting at every step.
   c) Somewhere in between.

15. **Do you have a diary/day book/wall chart, or**

   a) scrappy bits of paper and post-it notes everywhere?
   b) always looking for a better system?
   c) just given up?

16. **What do you do with unwanted material?**

   a) I hang on to everything "*just in case*".
   b) I have a huge recycling bin and shredder, which are my pride and joy.

17. **Is your desk a bombsite or is the top unmarked, polished perfection?**

   a) Spotless.
   b) I can't get my feet under the desk for the overflow of files and papers.

18. **What about the rest of your workspace?**

   a) organised and clear.
   b) a total mess.
   c) I have to dodge tottering piles of documents and folders to get to my desk.

19. **Do you have adequate storage furniture (cupboards, shelves, etc.)?**

   a) just what I need.
   b) not really. (Time to take action?)

20. **Are you always looking for new methods of filing and storage?**

   a) I've just given up.
   b) I have a scheduled time to sort out any mess and plan next steps.

21. **How do you work with others (co-workers/external contacts)?**

    a) always have good relations.
    b) a bit prickly.

Look back over your answers and you should get a clear insight into your organising needs, which you'd always known deep down and not necessarily admitted to yourself.

The next action is to look at the next section, '**Your work style personality**', to identify your particular work style, as this has a significant impact on your effectiveness.

When you have done this:

- List in your workbook, all items which you identify with and consider to be problems.

- Match these to the topics in the sections '**How to be more organised**' and '**Sorting out your office problems**'.

As you look through those two sections, look for any other areas where you think you might potentially have some organising problems, and note these in your workbook.

YOUR WORK STYLE PERSONALITY

Everybody has their own '*work style personality*'.

This section describes the main work styles, so that you can go through them and find the one which fits you most closely. This will give you some insight into what you might need to change about the way you work.

The speed demon

You do everything FAST. Whether it's a new idea, driving a car, or writing a report - you're OFF.

You love email because of its demand for instant attention, and you always respond immediately: no printing it off and thinking about it; action is your by-word.

You thrive on crisis, being busy, being on-the-go, and doing more than one thing at a time. Multi-tasking was created with you in mind.

You have a high energy level, are outgoing and sociable, good at networking, and probably work in sales or some form of customer service. However, you're irritated by people who respond more slowly. You're often impatient with other styles, particularly the **ponderer** (shown below), as your attitude circulates around the notion of "*What's there to think about? The action needed is clear, so let's get on with it.*", but sometimes your lack of thinking things through can make you too impulsive.

You rush through tasks or short-cut procedures to save time, but this can mean that you have to re-do details you've botched in your hurry. Sometimes you need to judge which tasks need more careful attention and slow down a little.

You're good at personal relations, so you follow-up and keep in touch with your network.

You sometimes have trouble focusing on the present, as you're off and away to the next important item on your list. Constantly moving on means that you sometimes miss what's happening now.

The ponderer

You're someone who enjoys thinking and examining questions from many angles. This means you're a slow decision-maker and make no decision unless you're completely certain it's the right choice for you.

You like books, papers and any information that will give you confidence. This thoughtful approach makes you strong, careful and attentive. However, sometimes your careful steady approach can have its drawbacks for effective working practice.

The problem is that you love information, have lots of it, and so you work in a cluttered space which is full of old, maybe outdated, material. You can't let go, as you need everything at your fingertips. Your tendency to make slow decisions means that clutter isn't moved out, and so you constantly remain snowed under.

The result of this way of working may be that you have so much clutter that you can't find information when you need it, which is ultimately counter-productive.

The procrastinator

You plan to think about and do things - tomorrow.

You're a habitual procrastinator, always putting things off without considering the effects of a delayed action or decision. For you, this is the default way of handling even simple and unimportant tasks. You prefer to do something more exciting and fun, and ultimately believe it will be easier to do later - which it won't.

This approach has some serious effects on your success:

- It affects your effectiveness, and your ability to complete work as and when agreed.

- Your personal life also suffers, as you also behave this way outside work, and

- Your reputation suffers, as you fail to deliver on your commitments.

Procrastination is a major area you need to improve. It has become the easy way to operate, but has tremendously bad effects on your work.

The visual worker

You have to see things to remember to act on them or remember where they should be. Your office is engulfed with papers, files, boxes and folders.

In fact, you won't file anything, as you believe you'll never find it again. Your walls are covered with reminders, white boards, tacked-up sheets and records of events you've attended. You remember where things are by visualising what they look like or which pile they're in. This is an unreliable method, and so you're constantly searching for missing items.

Visual personalities are often artists, designers, engineers and musicians, whose energy, originality and style are a great benefit to colleagues - but there are many challenges for you. For example, you have a hard time locating anything specific, because having everything always visible makes clutter the norm. Your main challenge is to find a way to keep things visible, but orderly and easy to find.

You believe that if it's not within sight, it's lost, despite there being areas of your life - such as in your kitchen - where you can't see everything, but they still function without a problem. The same results can be achieved in your office by using the right organising methods.

The sensitive worker

You value calm, peace, order and open clean spaces, and you feel stressed when there is physical chaos. Because you can't stand disorder, you look as if you're in a state of total order, but heaven forbid that someone opens any drawers and cupboards, or they'll see that everything has been shoved away out of sight.

This is rather like a teenager having a quick tidy-up of their bedroom. Everything's out of sight but can't be found afterwards.

You might even have bought organising tools, in an attempt to bring order and simplicity into your office, but you've never understood how they should be used. You need a more focused approach, not just to push things out of sight.

The combination worker

You might not have a single primary work style but instead include aspects of various styles, which you use in different circumstances.

You may be a **speed demon**, who is also **visual** with a slight degree of the **ponderer**'s care (now and again), or maybe even a **procrastinator** with visual tendencies who has to have some things piled up.

A combination is the most common profile, and your challenge is to keep in mind your goal - which is, ultimately, to move from being stressed, harried and confused, to being focused and productive.

Summary

Consider each aspect of your work style and how it affects your working practices, particularly your ability to be organised. What behaviour do you need to modify, to become more organised in your office?

> You need to:
>
> - become aware of how you do what you do – your *'work style personality'*.
>
> - recognise what aspect of your work style is stopping you from being better organised.

Discovering what is unsatisfactory about the way you work gives you a starting point for deciding what you can do to improve.

Why am I so disorganised?

What else affects my ability to be organised?

Many other factors affect your ability to be organised. These include the following:

TASK OVERLOAD

Not so long ago, every office had specialists to keep everything in the office running smoothly. Now there are fewer secretaries, filing clerks, computer specialists and technicians to maintain basic office services.

In the home office, this is particularly true, as you have to deal personally with every maintenance job and crisis, if you are to keep everything running smoothly.

Technological developments now mean that you have to do several jobs within your own job, such as needing to manage your diary, attending meetings, responding to your acquaintances, typing, filing as well - all in addition to doing your actual work.

Furthermore, you also have to be office manager and technical support. Doing so many jobs as well as the 'real job' means that you often have an overload, so it's no wonder you despair of ever getting on top of the office admin.

INTERRUPTIONS AND DISTRACTIONS

You can reduce these by being aware of what's distracting you, and for what length of time.

Concentrate on making distractions as brief as possible, even if you're tempted by the sunshine or the latest gossip.

PROCRASTINATION

However much we become organised, procrastination can be our biggest time-stealer. What's distinctive about this is that we are at our most original and creative when justifying why we haven't done what we had seriously intended to do. Instead of reasons, we are really giving excuses.

Read more on avoiding procrastination in the section '***Sorting out your office problems***'.

BELIEFS

No matter how strong your purpose, if you hold beliefs that are at odds with it, you won't succeed.

What do you really think about being disorganised? Perhaps you really enjoy messiness? Find it easier to leave things around than clear them away?

The surprising reality is that most creative, innovative and productive people are impeccably neat and orderly.

Remember that becoming organised isn't a simple once-and-for-all event, but is actually a system which you develop over time and then begin to use constantly. As part of this process, at different times different aspects of organising will be the most important.

Once you understand that the organising cycle is a constantly evolving process, you can then adjust the emphasis to meet your current needs.

BAD HABITS

Habits take a long time to form, so changing a habit won't happen overnight. We disorganised people have a low regard for the discipline of returning things to their proper place so that they're where we can find them next time we need them. Instead, we create false reasons (or 'excuses') such as: "*There's no point in putting it away, as I might need it soon*".

We have created our bad habits of disorganisation. The more often we do it the wrong way, the more the 'habit' becomes the only way to do it.

Once you stop telling yourself that creating order is of 'minor' importance, the sooner you'll be able to attend to what matters, because you won't be rushing around in an "*I can't find it!*" panic.

You will find out more about how to change habits in the next sections.

> **A FINAL THOUGHT**
>
> Becoming organised involves three elements:
>
> - Your **conscious self** - What am I doing?
>
> - Your **unconscious self** - What's driving me to behave this way?
>
> - The **external world** – Where will I get support?
>
> These are the factors that contributed to the making of your non-organised self, and each must be included in the creation of the new 'organised you'.

Part 2

How to be more organised

Must sort out this mess!

Organise your home office

How to be more organised

Now you understand more about why you're disorganised, you're ready to start on the road to becoming better organised.

Every day, everywhere, there are people (just like you and me) who accept what seems to be inevitable: that they'll always be in a mess. This is not true. Now that you know the nature of your disorganisation, you're ready to start putting it right.

What could get in your way and stop you from using this opportunity to become more organised?

- familiarity - sticking to what you know (your comfort zone),

- the imagined risk, danger and challenge of the unfamiliar and unknown,

- lack of belief that you have the ability to change how you do what you do.

To change how you organise your office, you need to create a workplace and a way of working which is created **by you** especially **for you**. It must complement your preferred way of working.

It must be a place where you're able to remain focused and in control, and see organising as just another part of your work.

53

It will make an enormous difference to your success, when you have created a workplace which is:

- organised,
- controlled,
- calm,
- focused,
- pleasing.

In your perfect workspace, you can do:

- what you want,
- when you want,
- how you want.

Remember: the purpose of this book is to enable you to create a place and a way of working which leads to success.

Why do you want to be organised?

You probably know a lot about what you don't want in your life, but what do you actually **want**? It's not only the detail of what you want which is vital, but a clear view of the **reason** why you want to be organised will give you:

- determination,

- commitment,

- motivation,

- focus.

Being disorganised drains you, because you are constantly hunting for lost items, making plans that aren't achieved, and scrambling to meet deadlines you don't reach.

Until now, you haven't got yourself organised, because you feel it's a waste of time and energy, as you feel powerless in the face of all the chaos around you.

The good news is that you created this mess through your choices and actions, so you can take back power over the world of your home office by taking fresh action.

Organise your home office

Seven steps to an organised you

You will become super organised by following these seven steps...

STEP ONE: FIND YOUR PURPOSE

Ask yourself:

- Why do you want to be organised?

- What is your disorganisation stopping you from being, having or doing?

- What do you hope to achieve by being organised?

Write these answers in your workbook. This will give you some ideas about how disorganisation is affecting you, and the benefits of improving how you work.

In your workbook, complete the following sentences:

- When I'm more organised, I will experience more...

- When I'm more organised, I will have more...

- My disorganisation prevents me from...

The next exercise will show you what you will gain from being organised:

In your notebook, complete the following sentences:

- When I can find things easily, I will...

- When I stop rushing about, I will feel...

- When I get rid of my backlog, I will...

- When I work in a beautiful space, I will...

- When I've cleared my desk, I will...

You can now see the value to your life of being organised, and the good effects which will result.

STEP TWO: CREATE YOUR VISION OF THE FUTURE

You need to create a vision of how you want your office to function.

- In your notebook, write a detailed description of how your office works now.

- Now describe your ideally organised office in your workbook. How does it work? What's in it? What do you do in it and how?

- Choose a role model (real or fictional) who's well organised – who do you know who you'd like to copy?

Go over your answers from these exercises, and work out what being more organised would add to your life.

Take a new page in your workbook and note key words and phrases from the exercises. What's repeated? What jumps out as being important?

Take these key points and list them as *"By being organised, I would…"*

Finally, write a summary beginning *"My reasons for being organised are…"*

STEP THREE: YOUR EXCUSES FOR BEING DISORGANISED

Excuses or 'reasons' are lies you tell yourself to justify not changing how you work. This is the lazy way out of making necessary changes. You're really short-changing yourself by making excuses for inaction, as this means that you will miss out on the opportunity to benefit from re-organising your home office.

So take yourself in hand and be bold enough to review your current situation:

- What do you do that creates chaos? Describe it in as much detail as you can.

- What does your disorganisation cost you?

- What are the thoughts that lead you to create a mess? e.g. *"I've always been a messy person"*.

Here's more on the excuses, or 'reasons', you tell yourself. Look at this list. Which ones have you used?

- I don't mind the mess – it doesn't bother me

- I've been like this so long I can't change my ways.

- Everyone is like this.

- I don't see the point of cleaning up. It'll only get messed up again.

- Piles of papers are OK – I can soon find what I want underneath.

- I'm just naturally lazy and untidy.

- I'm just easily distracted.

Now, give up those beliefs which limit what you can do, by remembering aspects of your life where you're **good** at organising yourself. Your car/garage? garden? hobby? charity work? holidays? running a club?

Summarise, in your workbook, any areas of life where you're able to organise yourself effectively.

What is it you do there, which is different from in your home office?

This will give you a picture of what you do right, which you can transfer to your office.

Record your answers, and note that your beliefs about being disorganised are not true everywhere in your life. Keep anything negative and unhelpful off the page - and out of your mind.

Remind yourself:

- I can be really well organised.

- I can handle interruptions and get back on track.

- I can cope with whatever crops up.

If you support these positive statements with a picture in your mind of being organised and in charge, it will happen.

The work of re-organising yourself has two parts:

1. Knowing the detail of **how** you do it.

2. Reminding yourself constantly: "I'm as capable of being organised as I want to be".

You need both.

Now look at the cost of disorganisation:

- In your notebook, write down everything your disorganisation costs you: Money? Disruption of your personal life? Your professional reputation?

What do you dislike about your current behaviour?

- Ask yourself: What will you gain when you've become a more organised you? Money? Time? Love? Friendship? Success?

- Describe in detail how much better your life will be when you deliver good work on time, e.g. feel more relaxed? Have more mental and physical space for ideas? Be more creative, more patient, more responsive, more positive?

- Make a commitment to yourself to make being organised a transforming element in your life.

Take time over this activity - start it and leave your workbook out where you can see it, and keep adding to the list.

Step Four: Set your organising goals

What do you want to achieve by being organised?

Although the answer can seem straightforward, it can also look daunting and overwhelming, because your personal sabotage gremlin (which we all have) tip-toes out of its hidey-hole and whispers words of self-doubt:
  "You'll never do it" or *"It's too much effort"*
Refuse to pay any attention!

You need to:

- Set goals

- Plan action

- Create support

Consider what you need to do, to establish goals for your journey towards achieving 'organised you'.

Now you're ready to set your goals (which are also called objectives or aims).

The key to success in goal-setting has two steps:

1. Create a mental picture of your goals. What does it look like, sound like, feel like?
2. Make a plan for achieving these goals.

You need to set out with your purpose clear or you're almost certain to go off-track.

By declaring your intentions, you tell yourself that you know exactly what you're aiming for, which makes success much more likely. Now, what do you need, in order to achieve your goals?

Read on for details.

STEP FIVE: METHODS FOR BECOMING ORGANISED

This section will show you how to

- clear backlogs.
- build new systems and habits.
- improve your time management.
- clarify and stick to your goals.

You need to be clear about your goals (see previous step) so that you can decide on your priorities. Then make sure that the high priority tasks take more of your time than low priority/non-urgent actions.

Sort your tasks

Sort your tasks into the following four categories, using the examples to help you:

A = important and urgent

B = important but not urgent

C = urgent but not important

D = neither urgent nor important

A: IMPORTANT & URGENT
B: IMPORTANT - NOT URGENT
C: URGENT - NOT IMPORTANT
D: NOT URGENT OR IMPORTANT

A Important and urgent

e.g. Finish preparation of presentation to the Board tomorrow (needs to be done NOW to be ready for the following day). This is where you should spend most of your time.

B   Important but not urgent

e.g. Create the plans for having an additional office abroad (important, but NOT needed now). This is important, but doesn't have quite the same urgency as the tasks in category A.

C   Urgent but not important

e.g. Routine correspondence which could have been done another day. Needs to be done, but not necessarily right now. Not central to the work - postpone this until you have finished category A.

D   Neither urgent nor important

Perhaps an email not meant for you, but which might be useful in the future. This is a complete time waster – if it's something for you, you'll get to hear about it some way. These tasks should only be considered if you need to pass the time (i.e. if there is nothing else to be done.)

Summary of task sorting

Essentially, you need to consider which of these categories you spend most of your time on now. If you're serious about getting on (whatever that means to you), you have to spend most of your time working in category **A 'Important and urgent'**. That's what will achieve success.

So - make up your mind where you want to get to, and understand the consequences of avoiding doing the tasks in category A, in favour of tasks in category D.

Learn to say "No"

If you always say "*yes*" to everything, then you'll have lost complete control of your schedule. You'll find that you're over-burdened, and you won't be able to carry out what you should be doing - which are, fundamentally, your main objectives.

By doing things that you don't have to do, in order to please others, you are at the mercy of their whims, instead of satisfying your own needs.

There are three ways of saying "**No**":

> **Aggressive**: Complain about being over-burdened and taken for granted, accuse the person making the request of being unreasonable, continue your rant and end up by slamming the door (recognise this?).
>
> **Timid (non-aggressive)**: Don't say "No", but turn your back, mutter to yourself and complain to someone nearby. From this, everybody loses, but you think that you have expressed your true feeling, however ineffectively, by doing it indirectly.
>
> **Assertive**: Express appreciation at being asked, but be effective by firmly explaining that you can't do it and giving a clear reason. The other person may not like it, but you've made your position clear without being rude. If they continue to ask, persist with statements such as "*I understand your difficulty, but I'm sorry, I can't do it*".

Which of these do you think is the most effective, in getting what you want and keeping people's respect?

Time Management

In your workbook, write down how you currently:

- spend your time,
- plan your activities,
- estimate task timings,
- track projects,
- meet deadlines.

The following section will help you to make these tasks easier.

You will find out below how to:

- plan your activities over different time periods,
- choose planning and tracking activities in a way that works for you,
- work out how long it takes to do a particular task,
- reduce your procrastination,
- track projects,
- meet deadlines by getting yourself organised.

The point of managing your time better is to work in a way which is:

- calmer,
- more relaxed,
- more effective.

Plan your work against different timescales.

The most common are a day, week, month, three months, or possibly a year. For each of these, you have to decide:

- your objectives,
- action needed to achieve them,
- how long you think each step will take,
- what help you need from others,
- an overall plan.

To get all the above done, you need to know how each project is working out.

For this, you need to keep track of:

- meetings and appointments,
- what's been done,
- what remains to be done,
- who's doing what for you and by when,
- when and how you should follow up others' agreed activities.

Planning each day and week.

- Set clear achievable targets.

- Use checklists of daily and weekly routines (see next exercise) so that nothing is missed.

- Break up your week with activities that involve contacts with other people, such as meetings and events, in order to maintain your networks.

- Ensure that your day includes contacts with family and friends.

- Do not become a solitary workaholic. Keep a varied schedule of activities. It's vital to understand that maintaining contacts is a vital part of your work.

- Don't be tempted to work in your pyjamas or tracksuit. Okay, there's nobody to see you, but it will affect your professional feeling and the level of serious attitude towards your work.

- Typing in bed on a laptop or on the patio in the sun will only make you nod off - leave that until the end of the day.

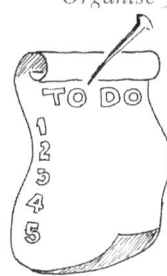

'To do' lists are essential.

Start with a MASTER list which shows the major projects in which you're involved for the next three months (or however long ahead you're planning).

Next, make sub-lists for every project. Each should show the project's detail, including all the tasks involved, with completion deadlines. This will give you a structure for each project.

For example, if you're organising a charity run, list every activity from now up to the end of the follow-up review, and include admin, finance and the role of everyone involved.

Use the project sub-lists to set up your checklists of daily and weekly routines.

It may all look impossible to complete, but having lots of sub-lists - each holding due dates for the completion of each key task - will provide a basic framework from which you will be able to shape your checklists and achieve each project.

Make sure your **daily checklist**:

- is clearly presented, even if it's hand-written.

- is in a place where you can find it easily - not dotted about on post-it notes or scraps of paper.

- only contains today's 'to do's.

- only contains activities which you think are manageable within the day.

Learn how to work SMART

What do you need in order to achieve your goals?

> You need to work **'SMART'**, which is short for:
>
> - **S**pecific
>
> - **M**easurable
>
> - **A**chievable
>
> - **R**esults, which are
>
> - **T**ime-related.

Specific means that your 'good idea' of becoming more organised has to be broken down into specific types of activity which you particularly want to improve.

You've identified these through the self-assessment you did earlier, and you will carry out these improvements by using the tools in the section *'Sorting out your office problems'*.

Measurable is a way of calculating whether you've achieved something. Each objective is just a 'wish list', which will never become reality, unless you use some method of measuring whether you've achieved your goal.

Measuring tools take two forms:

- **Subjective** assessment, by you or others, of a particular skill, such as using PowerPoint effectively for a presentation; or of a behavioural improvement, such as being assertive more often than aggressive or timid.

- **Quantitative** assessment of something like keyboard speed, which will give you records of speed and accuracy.

Achievable means setting objectives that require a stretch to achieve them, but are not unrealistic. Set a large goal, such as reducing the number of hours at your desk; then split it into achievable sub-goals, such as saying "No" more often, or delegating more.

The sub-goals should be critical to the achievement of the large goal and will give you positive feedback on success. Think big on major goals and small on sub-goals - that way you'll achieve what you intend.

Results oriented means that you always consider the outcome you want from any changes you make. By all means, stay an hour later to finish something, but if you're too tired to do anything useful during that hour, you haven't achieved the best result.

Every change must be linked to the achievement of an objective. You might feel like making improvements by clearing your workspace, buying new furniture or starting a different method of file storage and retrieval, but first consider how long it will take you to learn and use the new items, as the

pay-off has to be balanced against the **investment** of time and effort.

If learning a new procedure will take months, maybe you should use something simpler, or even adapt and improve your current system.

As time is the final frontier for these changes, the last item is...

Time-related. This brings in the key factor of "*It's all very well planning these improvements, but how am I going to manage what I have to do each day, as well?*"

The key to this is to give yourself deadlines and milestones along the way - it's amazing how a deadline stops you frittering away your time.

The word deadline comes from an ancient custom of killing someone who didn't cross the finishing line in a race within the expected time. Just be grateful that won't happen to you, if you don't finish in time.

Finally, objectives, goals or aims - whatever you call them - are simply **targets** for you to focus on. Think of an archery target or dartboard and imagine you're aiming for the bull's-eye. Set your goals in the context of **SMART** and you'll succeed.

Learn effective working habits.

The way you work and the unconscious habits you've formed have a key effect on your success, and so it will help you enormously to learn the best ways to work, which are:

- at the right time for you,
- in short bursts,
- using conscious habits as much as possible,
- systematically.

Furthermore, remember the key recommendation...

DO THE WORST FIRST.

This lets you get rid of the one task you're really dreading (e.g. that phone call / meeting).

Do that one horrible job first ("*I really don't want to make that call*") and whatever the outcome, it's DONE, and you can then re-focus without it hanging over you all day.

Learn to establish the most effective working habits:

- Keep your schedules for the next day, week, month and year up-to-date.
- Manage your workspace so that it's always clear and organised.

- Regularly and systematically, carry out your routine filing and computer housekeeping.

Keep these habits going by:

- **Repetition**: This works for learning any new skill, whether tennis or typing. In the same way, you can establish new good habits at work.

- **Reinforcement**: This involves mentally re-emphasising the benefits that you experience when you change your working habits.

Improve your decision-making, by recognising the two parts to making any decision:

- Clarify the process, then
- Identify your options.

Clarify the process by asking yourself:

- Why do I need to make this decision?
- What are the goals I want to achieve?
- What information do I need?
- What will happen if I don't do anything?
- Who do I need to involve?
- What's the timescale?
- What resources do I need?

Identify your options:

- Use brainstorming to identify all possibilities.
- Weigh the pros and cons of each option.
- Make the final choice.

The way you work will be improved if you:

- Tackle the tasks that place the greatest demands on you, at the time when you're most energetic.
- Maintain regular work habits.

STEP SIX: SUPPORT

Who could support you through your re-organising project?

Of all the people you know, what person or group springs to mind?

Remember, it's not necessarily the most loving or closest people to you who will give you the right sort of help. You will also need some 'tough love' to help you get rid of stuff (both physical and emotional) that you are reluctant to ditch.

Getting rid of familiar bad habits can leave you feeling naked and vulnerable. This encourages you to hang on to bad routines, if you're not challenged.

Consider:

- friends? family?
- previous/current colleagues?
- a professional organiser or coach?
- professional organising groups?
- a self-support group with others who are re-organising themselves?

Ask yourself what each of these people/groups could offer. Make sure to ask for help if some of the activities seem overwhelming.

People you know are more willing to provide support than you might imagine. Also, consider whether you can provide support for them – is there anything you can offer in return, so you create a kind of joint venture? e.g. tell them about your re-organising project and ask if you could help them with their office, in exchange for their support.

STEP SEVEN: THE FUTURE

Keep an eye on how you're doing and check whether anything's getting in the way, such as false beliefs like *"It's just too difficult for me."* If you find you've run up against buffers which are stopping you, contact an organising buddy or a support group.

Realise that organising is about creating your new organised space, which frees you from the effects of clutter so that you don't revert to chaos.

In your new world of being organised, you will find 'a place for everything and everything in its place', and you will have formed a place where you can create what's important to you.

Being organised means you can:

- find what you want when you need it,

- keep track of important information, so you can lay your hands on it easily and complete your work on time, without getting stressed,

- keep agreements,

- take action whenever you want to grasp new opportunities,

- focus on what's important to you.

By using the methods shown in this section, you will begin to see a lot more purpose and organisation in your life – and much less disorganisation.

Doesn't it feel good!

Organise your home office

Part 3

Sorting out your office problems

Getting there!

Organise your home office

There are a number of specific organising 'problems' when setting up a home office or working from home. This section deals with those topics in detail.

Arranging your office: the basics

> Firstly, ask yourself: How do you feel as you get ready to go into your office?
>
> - Excited, full of energy? Can't wait to get started? Love the place, because being there leads to great satisfaction and achievements? or...
>
> - Don't really want to be there, but suppose you must?

Are you fed-up with everything about the place? The machines and furniture, each of which has been on the list on to be repaired/replaced for so long that you've almost forgotten what you use them for?

Are you sick of tripping up on that torn rug? Have you had quite enough of staring at the sagging window blind?

Everything about where you work has an effect on your conscious and unconscious mind, your mood, and your ability to work and concentrate. This, in turn, affects how effective you are.

The whole place, from the seemingly trivial (there's that broken blind again), to the obviously vital (your computer) affects your performance and your view of how well you're doing.

Organise your home office

Staying focused on what's important (your goals/objectives) partly depends on how your office environment affects you. This includes everything you see, touch, smell and hear.

This ranges from your desk and chair (second-hand or the latest Milan design?), your storage method for files and folders (cardboard boxes or streamlined modern units?), to the smell of the office (fresh coffee or bad drains?)

Even the noise that filters through from outside affects you (tranquil, well-tended garden or loud traffic?). Are you someone who must have complete silence to work or someone who can only work if surrounded by your favourite music? Whichever you are, arrange to set it up the way that suits you.

Working in your office

Ask yourself:

- Do you have to keep getting up from your desk to get things that are out of reach?

- Is there a load of clutter on your desk or around your feet?

- Are you distracted by the mess, which irritates you but has become a permanent fixture?

- Do you suffer from backache, because you've never bothered to sort out whatever you need to make sitting at your desk more comfortable?

- Are you continually struggling with books, files, and folders, all of which are lying around and cause you to knock papers off your desk whenever you reach for something?

- Is your nickname Miss/Mister Messy?

- Are you continually searching for things that aren't where they should be?

- Are cupboards and bookcases crammed with stuff you don't want, don't need, don't like and will probably never use? Can't remember when you last looked at any of it?

If your answer is a resounding "**YES**", you're making life difficult for yourself, and your first job is to create a simple system to clear the clutter:

> Find 3 boxes (of any kind) and mark them ...
>
>
>
> 1. **Chuck out**
> 2. **Pass on**
> 3. **Keep/Store**

Go through all the mess and sort everything by putting them into one of the boxes. Take the '**Chuck out**' box and empty it into a container for rubbish/recycling and...

THROW IT AWAY!

NB You will feel a strong urge NOT to throw away anything, so you will need a buddy to help with this job, preferably someone who is ruthless at discarding all the 'treasures' you're tempted to keep. Because your buddy doesn't have the same emotional attachment to these, it's easy for them.

You will then have the physical and psychological space to begin afresh and so you will be able to create a **new storage system,** which you will maintain and keep going, so you won't ever end up in such a mess again.

COMBINING WORK AND HOME

A unique feature of the home office is that it links work and home. It seems almost too obvious to mention, but that creates issues and difficulties that are in a different universe from those of the standard office.

No matter whether you're running a business from home, studying, arranging events, or keeping family schedules organised, you will be in conflict with domestic routines. However far away you locate yourself, domestic matters will still intrude and seep into your territory, in the form of the dog visiting or your daughter's piano practice.

Combining work and home requires new rules and agreements, which means that you need to create new routines, such as regular family meetings, to enable glitches to be spotted before they become serious problems. Disagreements about clutter and time may seem to be surface issues, but they reflect one of the central questions about sharing a joint space.

This probably goes back to pre-history, but the issue of space-sharing and territory is as much of an issue in the present day.

The strong emotional response of *"Get out of my way!"* has evolved from *"Get out of my cave!"* This shows our need to shape our space and mark our territory - whatever we're doing.

The rule that should be agreed is that anything in the office stays there and is not moved to other parts of the home or used there.

If you don't apply this rule and enforce it, you will get 'office creep', which results in bits of the office appearing in every part of your home, with the laptop always on the kitchen table, stationery in the hall, and notepads being in the dining room.

Furthermore, using your lap-top in front of the TV invades others' space, although it's common practice. You need to keep working activities separate from leisure and social times.

HOME-BASED DISTURBANCES

Here are some ways to reduce the effects of interruptions wherever you work:

- Keep a record of the main causes of disturbance, e.g. certain time-wasting people, phone calls... and consider ways of tackling the problem, such as banning visitors or directing calls to ansaphone, at certain times of the day.

- Cluster tasks such as phone calls and emails, instead of doing them one at a time. This fools your brain into believing it's a single job, so you won't feel overwhelmed.

- Disable the instant notification of emails or voicemail messages, and deal with them at fixed times that you've set yourself.

- Phone back at times of the day when people are less likely to extend the conversation, or schedule a time between appointments.

- Assign yourself a time slot each day which is known as the "*do not interrupt me*" time, which should coincide with the time of day you are at your best. First, you need to discover whether you're a morning, afternoon or evening person.

CREATING YOUR PERSONAL HOME OFFICE SPACE

Keep the two key areas of your life (office and personal) as separate as possible. You could do this, for example, by installing a second phone line, so that there is no overlap between personal/domestic and work calls. This can also include separate voicemail.

- Identify the nature of your work and your requirements.

- List the types of task you will be performing (phoning / word processing / designing?).

- Consider the furniture and equipment you need.

- Should the office include a space for colleagues / clients / customers?

- Consider where is the best place for your office: spare bedroom? basement? kitchen? garden shed?

You need to take yourself seriously as someone working from home, and this means the creation of a professional environment, which may not be large or grand, but must ultimately be right for its purpose.

It should provide a combination of comfort and professionalism which will enable you to focus on your work.

REDUCING PROCRASTINATION

You might use this behaviour in every part of your life, but we're just looking at it in the context of your home office. Note that any strategies for overcoming procrastination here can be applied everywhere else.

Write a list of your **most disliked activities** and how you successfully avoid doing them by using a number of clever (if not exactly subtle) strategies, such as:

- 'forgetting' what you're supposed to do,
- starting tasks but leaving them unfinished
- just not doing what you've promised/intended

Can you add any other avoidance strategies you use?

What do you think is the **price** you pay for your avoidance strategies, e.g. not being trusted? Gaining a reputation for unreliability?

How much does this affect your success?

Mark beside each item on your list, a number corresponding to one of the three choices below:

1. Dump it
2. Delegate it
3. Do it

First, get rid of anything that's not inspiring you. Use phone calls/emails to free you from obligations, people and projects who/which aren't working for you. This should clear a lot of space for new, more exciting, projects to develop.

Next, delegate anything you're not excited about doing, e.g. find someone to do your tax return and book-keeping or anything that saps your energy. You could offer skills exchange instead of paying: *"I will do this for you, if you do that for me"*. More about delegation, later in this section.

Then, think about what you **really** want to do: something that **inspires** and **stimulates** your imagination.

Of course, there are many things you need and want to continue doing, but ask yourself what else you could focus on. In your diary, mark items to complete within the next three months.

Do it. You've cleared the stuff cluttering your life and are now free to spend time on what matters to you.

More tips for avoiding procrastination:

- Assemble everything you need before you start a project or piece of work.

- Break down each task into manageable chunks.

- Create a fake interim deadline, to keep you focused.

- Begin with either the easiest or the most difficult part, depending on your preferred way of working.

- Keep nibbling away at doing it, as this will keep you making progress.

- Get a 'procrastination buddy' and exchange stories, strategies and support.

- Watch out for self-imposed distractions - do you really need to make that call right now?

- Let others know when you need quiet time on your own (tell them your "*do not disturb"* period).

- Work at quiet times such as early morning or late evening.

GETTING TASKS DONE

Tasks always have unexpected elements. Happily, some work will be smooth and simple and take less time to complete than expected, but other tasks are sure to take up far more time than you anticipate. Of course, the 'quicker than expected' tasks may counteract the effect of the 'longer than expected' tasks, so that your schedule may remain as planned.

On a 'to do' list, be sure to group together minor tasks, such as phone calls, into half-hour slots, and allow extra time for interruptions or anything urgent which might come up (e.g. that phone call you're waiting for, offering you a million-pound contract).

However, having planned as much as possible, do remain flexible and able to deal with whatever the day throws at you.

As you create your short-term and long-term 'to do' lists, you will need to pull items from the master list you generated and insert these into your action list. The path of a 'to do' item should then look like this:

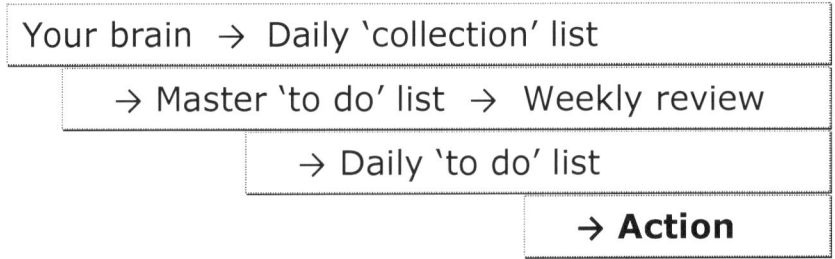

Delegating

When you have an activities overload, your best option is to delegate, or even to out-source a particular piece of work, as this reduces your load and gives someone else the responsibility.

This is an excellent idea, but there is a danger that you might spend so much time selecting, briefing, training, coaching and monitoring performance that you may ultimately **add** to your overload, instead of reducing it.

With this in mind, a key method of delegation is not to pass on the work to a junior, but to a colleague - someone equal in terms of training and knowledge. This is called '**sideways delegation**': working between colleagues at a similar or equal level.

In order to effectively delegate - whether to a junior or a colleague, depending on what you decide - you need to go through a series of standard steps which have been previously agreed.

For a **small business**, you will have to buy-in assistance, whether it's an IT agency, office services or a firm of cleaners. Cost-in these services to your business, into your budget estimates, as it's not efficient to try to do everything yourself.

If you're a student, sharing joint aspects of the work with a fellow-sufferer reduces your load.

1. **Decide what you will delegate**: Choose something that another person can do more quickly, more expertly or more cheaply than you, and which can be easily incorporated within their existing job - although this might inadvertently test your negotiating skills.

2. **Choose the right person**: For in-house delegation, it's tempting to select the most willing person who always obliges, but consider choosing someone who will benefit from the experience as a developmental activity. This will give you a new assistant who can become useful to you in the long-term, as well as easing your current load.

3. **Set up the arrangement**: For in-house delegation, ensure that colleagues - as well as the chosen person - clearly understand their responsibilities, authority and support, or there will be resentment and uncertainty making the rounds. The task has to be presented as an opportunity from which everyone benefits, and this should be done using all the communication media available.

4. **Stand back**: You've set it up in such a way that everyone knows what's happening. Be clear about the nature of any support you will provide, and don't interfere in the detail of the work or you'll find yourself with an even bigger overload. Mistakes need to be made for the person to learn, so keep out of the way. You can set it up as a mentoring or coaching opportunity, which would involve an agreement on review and feedback sessions, in which the experience will be examined together.

Informal encounters: As well as all the possible formal arrangements, some of which are shown above, there are also those informal and unexpected encounters which comprise much of the challenge, fun and excitement of organisational life (and often help to reduce the boredom).

It's well known that chance meetings over the water fountain, a hot photocopier or in a corridor can have more effect than planned formal events. The grapevine is alive and well, and flourishes in the most unexpected places. Gossip is often the place where truth is lurking, so don't stay aloof.

Organise your home office

Reading and writing

These skills have been part of your life since childhood and you use them every day, so why are they included here?

The reason is that although the way you use them at work isn't very different, sometimes there's an unexpected emphasis or a different use, so we need to look at how to use these skills effectively for different purposes.

One difference is that is that you use some kinds of documents often (e.g. 'to do' lists), others hardly at all (such as hand-written notes) and some fairly frequently (for example, a summary of a meeting).

Although reading and writing are separate sets of skills, they go hand in hand. Because they're so closely linked, they're presented together, in order to show that they complement each other, and go together 'like a horse and carriage', as the song says.

It therefore makes sense that you can complete both of these tasks as effectively, productively, and time-efficiently, as possible.

TIPS FOR MORE EFFECTIVE READING

- First, get a feel for the content by visually scanning the whole document. Follow this by using a highlighter pen to mark headings and subheadings and noting in the margin any keywords you spot.

- Now read carefully the first and last paragraphs of each section or chapter. Taken together, they will show the main points of the document. You will soon realise that you have an overview of the whole document, and you can then scribble notes in the margin, highlighting significant parts.

- Follow this with a brief (5-10mins) writing session, using your highlighted parts and rough notes to write in your workbook the bones of a summary. You'll be surprised how well you have grasped the meaning of the document.

NB You can use this method for anything from essay preparation to press coverage of a particular issue.

If you have a document which is a single piece of text without subheadings (which happens often), you will have to create your own headings.

Do this by noting the title and the beginning and ends of paragraphs, as these usually tell you:

- what the paragraph is about.
- any conclusions.

Together, these should give you enough to construct your own summary of the content.

Sorting out your office problems

- Mark any complex or difficult passages, and give them extra attention, so you really understand it all.

- Keep in mind the question "*What do I want to get from this?*" as this will help you to keep focussed.

- If you're sent a document you know nothing about, don't chase-up the sender. They will contact you if necessary – leave the responsibility for action on them.

- Don't attempt to read everything that's sent to you. Choose only those items that add value to your work, and be selective about what you put into your 'read later' pile, as this can become overwhelming.

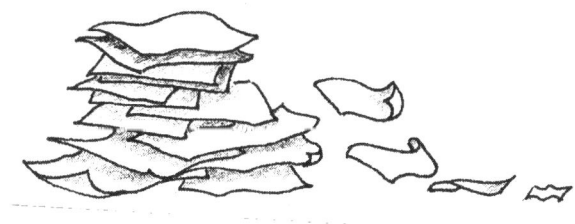

Check your reading file. Is it a teetering stack of dust-covered journals and books?

If so, schedule a regular clear out and dump anything out of date. See more detail on how to do this, in the section '***Paperwork Mountain***'.

103

TIPS FOR MORE EFFECTIVE WRITING

- **Get started**. However difficult and intimidating it looks, it won't go away, so **do something - anything** - about it. Make notes, scribble an idea for a structure - anything!

- The reason for taking action is that **activity** stops whatever is keeping you stuck, because getting started shuts up the negative inner voice. This gremlin that everyone has, creates a kind of writer's block which doesn't have any basis in reality. Whatever it says is untrue and any action you do shuts it up, so **get moving**!

- Give yourself **deadlines** and make them part of your day - use an alarm or timer to keep you on time, as you might wander off onto doing other things. You could also give yourself little rewards for reaching a goal, or perhaps a minor penalty for procrastination.

- Break the material into chunks and get ready for writing by choosing a particular period of time to complete it. Find a place where you won't be interrupted and put an 'out of bounds' notice on your door.

Use these **writing guidelines**:

- Keep memos short, no more than one page, and make sure you send information, not a discussion.

- Keep writing simple and to the point.

- Put a short **summary** at the beginning of a long document.

- Don't use wordy headings.

- Use spacing lines between paragraphs.

- Maximum of ten words per line.

- Maximum of **one** idea or subject per paragraph.

- Use different font type and sizes to give emphasis - but not too many.

- Use graphics and illustrations as much as possible, to break up dense blocks of text.

- Use subheadings to lead the reader through the text.

- When you think you've really done the best you can, take a last critical look and ask yourself: "*Does this look tempting to read? Is it easy to follow?*"

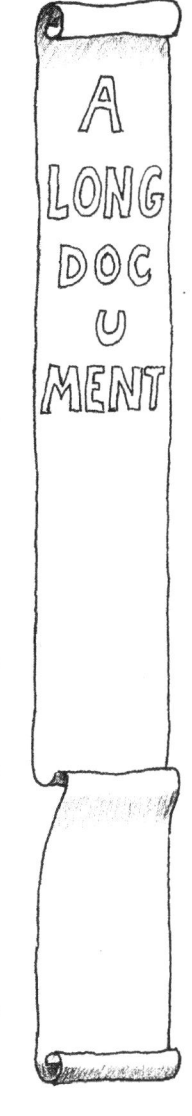

TIPS FOR EDITING

- **Get an overview.** Is the structure clear, with headings and subheadings? Does it look attractive? Is there plenty of white space between sections? Is there a summary at the beginning? Is there a clear table of contents?

- **Preview.** Does the structure make sense? Is it easy to follow? Are there any gaps in the meaning? Is there a glossary of difficult terms and an index, if needed?

- **In-view.** Does the style flow? Is it easy to follow? Is there any unnecessary jargon? Is any of it ambiguous?

- **Review.** Are the spelling and punctuation correct? Pages and tables numbered?

TIPS FOR IMPROVING YOUR MEMORY

With very few exceptions, everybody (including you) forgets up to 80% of what they've read within 24 hours. This has a number of negative effects, including the tendency to keep too many documents.

- Remembering is usually a form of association, so when reading, keep in mind a key question such as *"What will remembering this help me to do?"* or *"How does this fit with what I already know?"*

- To help you remember a document's contents, look carefully at the headings and subheadings, to get a picture of what it's about. From this, it's relatively easy to recall major points, and the detail will then come back.

- Write a summary or make notes in the margin, so that you will be reminded of the content when you next read it. (See the section *'Tips for more effective reading'* for more detail.)

- Read the material again 15-20 minutes later, and to fix it even more strongly in your mind, read it again a week or a month later (like exam revision).

- Usually, you will simply need to remember that it exists and where to find it, hence the importance of filing and retrieval.

Organise your home office

Paperwork mountain

How are you handling the BUMPH plague?
Every office the world over, whether it's a mega-corporation or a home-based office, is besieged with bumph, which has become a form of insidious international disaster.

Bumph can be defined as:

'Documents or information, which may be useful or look interesting, but that are either extremely longwinded or have arrived without being requested'

Because of their attention-grabbing appearance, you're tempted to look at them on arrival and even spend some time reading them through. This is your downfall.

You may recognise that you are becoming buried in a bumph snowstorm, if you can relate to many of the following:

- You often feel overwhelmed by the quantity of documents,

- find many uninviting to read or difficult to follow,

- constantly have to re-read a paragraph or page,

- struggle when making notes about a document,

- have poor concentration and are easily distracted,

- don't know which document to deal with first,

- can't easily extract important information from a document,
- don't always understand what you read.

You need to secure a good understanding of your paperwork, and be able to:

- select and understand what you need,
- connect new information to existing knowledge,
- retain and recall that information.

Question: How do I cope with piles of paper?

Answer: Sort them into five groups:

1. **Urgent** - give immediate attention and action.
2. **Complete within the next few days** - read or collect more information.
3. **Put aside** – not needed for a week or so. Put it on the back burner.
4. **Long-term** - attention required at intervals.
5. **Not needed** at all. Chuck these straight away.

From this, organise your daily paperwork into two categories:

1. Immediate attention and action required.

2. Read or collect more information.

Question: How do I decide what to bin?

Answer: Ask yourself what you really need, by matching material you're sent to your goals, i.e. would this item help you to progress to what's important? If it's not a "*how interesting!*" item, then it's probably useless bumph, so bin it.

Ask these simple questions about every piece of communication — electronic, paper or even spoken to you.

- Does this relate to a key part of my work?

- What could happen if I ignore it?

- How serious could that be?

- Do I need this now, or could I find it in the future?

- Do I want this at all?

Then, pose the final 'killer' question:

- What's the worst that would happen if I ignore it?

If your answer does not show you being fired, killed or becoming bankrupt, then it's probably OK to ignore it.

INFORMATION MANAGEMENT

Should you handle each document only once?

This is a view which is promoted by many time-management systems. In reality, however, this seldom happens - and often shouldn't.

There you are, creating a complex document which requires you to use lots of material you've collected; you're surrounded by various documents - some you'll use, others you'll reject but most need to have some attention - and finally, after handling various documents many times, you end up with the creation of a new document.

Usually there here are four stages of information management:

1. Reading,

2. Storing,

3. Retrieving,

4. Storing it again.

In order to categorise each piece of information and to understand quickly what you should do with it, you need to improve your speed of reading and understanding.

Whatever the size and importance of the document, there is a standard procedure for reading it more quickly and dealing with it.

1. Scan the document (read it quickly). This gives you a mental framework on which you hang the rest. This is called a preview, or the context.

2. If it's a long document, look at the title, contents, introduction and summary. There may not always be all of these, but whatever there is, use it to get as much of a document overview as you can.

You will now be able to ask yourself two questions:

- Which category is it? **Junk** / **Important** / Uncertain? - Take appropriate action.

- What do I need from it?

3. Now flick through the document, looking for section headings, structure, summaries. Look at the first and last paragraphs of each section or chapter, which will give you more detail of the content. Read the parts you need, in more detail.

See more tips below, under 'Reading and Writing'.

To help you to remember documents, use two methods:

- Recall the main points and general idea of key documents by **keeping notes** about them, either in a file on your computer, or in a physical workbook. Generally, it's best to do both.

- Summarise the main points or make **notes in the margin** — this will trigger your memory.

Sorting out your office problems

So long as you rigorously back-up your computer files, the need to physically store the documents in filing cabinets or folders in cupboards has almost disappeared. The only need for physical documents is for legal and tax purposes, unless it's something you frequently need when the computer is not available.

Nowadays, it's common practice to keep as much as possible in both electronic and hard copy. This is known as 'just in case' or defensive filing, so you won't be 'caught out'.

However, the reality is that only about 85 percent of documents stored in a filing cabinet are ever referred to again. To determine whether this applies to you, go through your current files, look at each document, and ask yourself these questions:

- When was the last time I looked at it?

- How long has it been sitting there untouched?

- Am I likely to be using it within the next six months?

- If it's part of the past, can I ditch it?

- Is it getting in the way or does it have any use?

- Will it have any use in the future?

Use these clutter-clearing questions for everything.

115

If you find your filing is dominated by 'keep just in case', try out a new approach by always asking yourself the questions above, especially

- What use will this document have in the future?

If your answer is still to be cautious, ask the second question,

- What's the worst that could happen if I lost it?

If the answer is not a version of "*my life would fall apart*", then ditch it.

CURRENT PROJECTS

Working on these every day means that you should keep them next to your desk. Mark each file for a particular purpose as you use it, such as reading for a meeting.

Don't just put them back in a tray, because you'll end up with piles of paper and you don't want your desk to become a general dumping area.

A simple way to keep track of live projects is to use a separate concertina file. This can also help with tracking, if you have a system where you record each time it's opened and what you've done.

Make sure that 'to read' files are kept separate and marked with a 'do by' date, otherwise they can become mixed up with general files. Remember to take the 'to read' files and actually read them.

REFERENCE FILES

These are items you need to refer to occasionally, such as material from current projects and activities. Before you finally store the material used in a project, weed out any rough drafts of working papers or you'll end up with very fat files with lots of redundant stuff.

Set up your filing system: decide on broad categories in which to group your files. These might include clients, customers, staff, projects, administration. Colour-code files in each category so that you can quickly cross-reference them.

Use alphabetical ordering for individual files within a category. Avoid the need to split large files which have grown within a very short time, by making sure you've got rid of all the unnecessary rubbish.

Now you can get down to 'serious filing'.

- Firstly, decide on the most suitable form of file container, e.g. box file, hanging file.

- Next, mark each file container with a precise name. If you're uncertain where to place it, consider the most likely context in which it will be required.

- Keep a list of current files next to your desk, so that you don't duplicate an existing file by creating a new one.

- Don't file hard copies of information that is already stored on a computer, unless you need to for legal reasons – duplication can make for more confusion than clarity.

- Make sure that there's a sensible directory structure for your computer files and always take a regular back-up, onto a different medium (e.g. a separate disc) in case the hard drive dies.

- **Do filing regularly**, so you don't have to wade through a large pile of documents – it can seem like yet another tedious chore, but it releases you from constantly hunting down a key file. Serious filing frees you from the tedium of searching, and releases you to do what matters.

- You need a simple tracking system; for example keep A4 cards next to the filing cabinet, each divided into three columns: file name, location and date filed/borrowed. Anybody borrowing or returning the file completes the card. This enables you to locate files when you need them.

- Electronic tracking of paper files: for example, Paper Tiger (*www.thepapertiger.com*) is a neat searchable database that allows you to designate different locations for information, e.g. reference files, document boxes, workbooks, for example. This is particularly useful for tracking information in various different types of location. Integration with Google Desktop is also provided.

PRUNING YOUR FILES

Managing files can easily become a huge job, as some items can become redundant in a matter of weeks, whilst others need to be kept for years.

Identifying what needs to be discarded or archived needs to be included in your long-term goals. Such an activity needs to be carried out every three months, so schedule regular file overhauls, which can either be a 'big bang' or a 'little and often' approach.

You need to be ruthless with the rubbish and not get tempted into reading files that are no longer your concern.

ELECTRONIC FILING

Storing documents electronically saves both time and space, and greatly helps in terms of sharing and retrieval of data. An electronic filing system is within the scope of any computer user, as all that's required is a scanner, the right software, and a storage device, such as a CD/DVD drive.

For the management of any scanned documents, there are many software products available, which provide both scanning and filing as well as retrieval. There are many current desktop search tools which can also be downloaded free of charge, e.g. from Google, Microsoft and Yahoo.

Organising computer files

You will need a simple and logical grouping of data which takes very little time but makes tasks like archiving straightforward. There will be many occasions when it's quicker to go directly to a subfolder where you know a file should logically be, than to attempt to recall a name or keyword in order to run a search.

Backing up

Make sure that you back-up files you have created, as the consequences of losing these can be unpleasant and serious.

PAPERLESS OFFICE

Taking modern information management to its ultimate electronic extreme, leads to the fully paperless office.

This doesn't suit everyone, as it requires you to:

- Keep up to date with technical developments in business-related areas,

- Make extensive use of speed reading,

- Keep learning and practising new useful techniques and software,

- Watch out for the dangers of falling into your comfort-zone, where you resist improvements.

The paperless office lets you do what you should be doing in your office – giving maximum attention to the work you're there to do and spending minimum time on routine activities. These should dealt with by a built-in system, which works but hardly needs any attention.

KEEP IN TOUCH – EVEN WHEN YOU'RE OUT

From the mobile phone to the newest all-singing and dancing gadgets (such as the I-Pad, I-Phone or Blackberry), modern technology can help you to keep in contact with your office, wherever you are, even if you are away for some time.

Summary of Information Management

Effective storage of information needs:

- a clear picture of what's worth filing and what to chuck out,

- a simple filing structure that is regularly reviewed and pruned of redundant material,

- The phrase **'back-up'** should be a key mantra at the end of the preparation of every document.

Part 4

Future action

Organised

Organise your home office

Future action

You've worked through the 'Organise Me' project and now you're going to continue with everything that you've decided to do - **Perhaps?**

The chances are that you're still working your way through your new actions and objectives. The sad reality is that good resolutions and intentions often disappear.

Remember the resolutions you make firmly every New Year? You move into January, sure they're going to happen, but come February they are fading away.

It's the same with this work. Whatever you've firmly decided to do differently, you can find that it slips away and your former bad habits take over — it's those sabotaging gremlins again.

A two-part strategy gets you through:

- having an **action plan**.

- maintaining a clear vision.

Now's the time to take stock, by reviewing and refining your tasks and objectives, adjusting priorities and setting new targets.

Your action plan

Go back to your workbook and check the goals you set yourself.

- Which of these have already been achieved? Give each one a big tick, which reminds you how well you've done.

- What amendments to your initial plans do you want to make, now that you've worked with the objectives and found things that work for you and things that don't? Carry out a review, in light of where you are **now**.

- Are there new areas of concern that weren't there at the beginning? If so, list them and go back to review the section '*Sorting out your office problems'*.

Your circumstances may be different now. If so, you need to establish new goals:

- Draw up an amended list of tasks and goals. Prioritise each on a 1-10 scale, according to your estimate of their importance.

- List each task, with target completion dates. Enter the tasks and dates into an action plan (as shown below).

My Action plan		
Main objective		
Sub-goals and targets	Start date	Target date

Review your progress weekly or monthly and give yourself a positive reward for every step forward, each of which acts as a springboard towards further achievement.

Importantly, don't be too hard on yourself if you don't achieve the rate of progress you expect. This may be because you're trying to achieve too many things at once, or because you haven't yet worked at it long enough to establish new habits.

However, don't abandon these new techniques just because there's a loss of momentum; instead, find ways to stay on track.

For example, you might start a weekly points system, with rewards and penalties for good and bad organisation. Points could be awarded for tasks, along the following lines:

- Add ten points for every day planned in advance.

- Subtract ten points for every 'to do' item carried forward to the next day.

- Subtract ten points for every task that someone else could have done.

- Add ten points for an empty filing tray at the end of the week.

- Subtract two points for every item still in your filing tray at the end of the week.

- Subtract two points for every email not dealt with on the day.

- Subtract two points for each additional day that you don't deal with it.

What if old habits re-appear?

Don't despair if you find that old habits sometimes return. Find the reason it happened, look again at the strategies shown earlier, set new targets and get back on track.

Getting (and staying) organised is for life, and needs resilience, determination and a positive attitude:

> Your motto is... *"**I can do it!**"*

Maintaining a clear vision

How do you picture your organising - right now and for the future?

See yourself with a clear office, an orderly filing system, with effective organising as part of your regular routine.

How does that look? What's going on? What is the atmosphere like? Is it calm and harmonious? What are you like in your office? What does it look like? What's wonderful about it? What are you achieving in this clear, orderly place?

Hang on to that image, and any time things go a bit wrong, go back to it in your mind to re-inspire you to continue.

Part 5

Examples and Resources

Snapshots of home office life

WORKING FROM HOME IS BEDLAM
(Adapted from the Guardian Weekend, June 9, 2007)

My house rocks and rolls as a place to work, sleep, eat and play. It's a four-bed semi and I live here with my wife, five kids, grandson and three dogs. I run an executive recruiting company, my wife runs a child-minding business from the conservatory, and it can be bedlam sometimes.

When I started working from home, I had a huge desk that went halfway round the dining room but I soon realised I didn't need all that. I converted the garage, adding a bar at a perfect height for me to write at, and the room becomes a party-place for the teenage children at weekends. In the school holidays, it can get very hairy with kids around and my grandson banging on the office door.

I don't need a desk and have a laptop, phone, fax machine and paperwork goes up into the loft. It's like living in two houses at once. When I finish in my office around six, that's it as I lock away my laptop, my wife puts the toys in boxes and all the kids are on a tidying rota. Within 20 minutes it's all done, as if you flip a switch and it turns into a different house.

This way of working has let me become self-sufficient and helps my home life so I can spend quality time here with the family.

ULTIMATE MULTI-TASKER

Because of the varied activities of my business, my office is spread all over the house. Following work as a food scientist in large companies, I set up as a specialist in diet-related activities and alternative health therapies.

I live alone in a small house in a modern development so, apart from the occasional lodger or long-term companion, I can use every room. As well as a phone in my office, I have an extension in my living room, where I can also take calls from clients and have all the paraphernalia for notes and appointment follow-up, as well as my A4 hard-back book, which I use as the basis for recording and tracking everything I do.

As my work concerns diet and food, I also have a place in the kitchen where I can spread out manuals and recipe information and record progress on projects. I use the conservatory for client consultations and also have a treatment room near my office for direct work with clients.

My office is organised into three distinct areas:

- a computer desk,

- an extra-wide writing desk and

- other multi-purpose surfaces.

The priority in my office is the maximum number of flat surfaces, which I need because my work involves many different activities.

Since I left employment, I have trained in related specialisms in the field of alternative health, such as aromatherapy and Reiki. Because of the variety of work, I find I need flat surfaces to lay out material I'm currently working on, which might be the preparation of a proposal, designing a diet programme or collating material for a workshop, so I also have folding tables which I can use.

For filing notes and technical information, I use ring-binder files and folders.

My greatest challenge is computer skills, as I'm not a natural teckie and can't keep pace with the rapid and frequent changes and developments in office technology, which is where I need support. For this, I pay a specialist or agree a skill exchange: "*You do this for me and I'll do that for you*", which works well for me, as I'm a natural networker.

Angela

SHARING THE OFFICE

The small Victorian terraced house I share with my husband doesn't provide the space we need to run our businesses. We each have part-time jobs as IT specialists as well as running small businesses, so the job of juggling priorities isn't helped by a lack of space in the house as well as all the IT technology objects lying about.

Reconciling our differing temperaments and needs is my major challenge. He needs constant music, but I need quiet and order, and so we have created separate 'offices', where we each use a laptop.

My space is the small patio (weather permitting), and his, the dining room, but the associated materials such as files and folders, proliferate and spread to every corner of the house, as does his favourite music, which is always playing. A result of this arrangement is that joint meals and social / quality time are almost impossible to organise, so the solution is not wholly satisfactory – perhaps I should move my office somewhere else, away from the house altogether, such as an office in a local business centre.

Denise

RELAXED AT WORK

I have a large house I share with my cat and I use all the rooms for different aspects of my work, but the central place is a special desk-chair, from which I phone, read, write up material, study and relax.

Previously, I worked in senior jobs in retailing but I became exhausted with the pressure and decided that self-employment would bring more satisfaction, control over my work and less stress. One year on, I have disciplined myself to set up effective systems so that there's no crisis management needed. Everything is smoothly running, as I buy-in support for domestic activities and chores such as tracking finance.

I constantly monitor how I'm doing, as continuous improvement is central to my business practice.

On a typical day, I make an early start, beginning with whatever I've prepared the evening before. This is followed by work, study, physical exercise and social contacts. I've found that the secret of smooth running is setting up and maintaining systems and procedures, so I never panic and work becomes a pleasure.

Renata

THE PAPERLESS OFFICE

When I started work as an engineer, I developed a love of simple and effective solutions to problems and decided to make maximum use of electronics and minimum use of paper.

I brought this approach to ultimate success when I managed a manufacturing plant in Vietnam, which employed 5000 people. I ran this without any paper systems, except for the finance department, which couldn't imagine not recording and storing everything on paper.

This paperless system worked in a third-world country recently past a major war, so I knew it must be simple to use in a western country full of highly educated and computer-literate people. For most people, the only obstacle in the way of working like this is your comfort-zone, in which you feel the need to see everything on paper instead of on a screen, for example by printing off emails.

Having left corporate life two years ago, I now run a number of businesses from home. These are mainly in the field of leadership and personal development and for this, I have an office in a former bedroom. In there, I use the maximum number of electronic devices, including three computers, two printers, a fax/scanner, using voice recognition software - no typing. Soon I will have the fax and computer linked, so there will be no need for paper copies there, either.

For meetings, I record everything on a digital recorder and I circulate action points, instead of minutes, making notes on a laptop at the meeting.

I use a headset for phone calls, so I can write notes at the same time and I usually have a learning tape playing to fill quiet moments.

Although I can have up to 100 emails a day, I speed-read my way through these and clear them in ten minutes.

Brian

OFFICE IN RETIREMENT

Since retiring from teaching, the activities in my office have become transformed. Before retirement, I used it to keep track of teaching preparation and admin, as well as recording and controlling sports activities, which were a major part of my job.

When I retired, I had to move my office to a distant part of the house, as my wife told me that she was sick of my work taking over the living room. I was banished to the attic, where I happily set up my office and now sit in resplendent solitude, in a sea of paper, electronic bits 'n' pieces and cameras, for the hobby which has now taken over much of my life.

I also spend time running sports activities for young people (I'll always be a teacher, I suppose) and arranging trips for us. Family events are jointly organised with my wife, who uses the office to record and keep track of plans.

As it's mainly my office, a great deal of the difficulty we had with my taking over house space has disappeared.

John

SOLO THERAPIST

Going solo as a therapist in the world of alternative medicine is challenging. Following a first career as a nurse, I trained as an alternative therapist after my children had grown up and left home. However, I hadn't realised that I would have to be a businesswoman too.

So there I was, fully qualified for my new career, but what next? I started by practising my new skills on volunteers drawn from family and friends, but was at a loss to know how to get myself established as a successful practitioner. Running a business isn't necessarily included in a therapist's training.

I started out by setting up a (very) basic home office in a corner of the landing and hung my framed certificates around my desk to remind me of what I'd trained to do. I then contacted others who had been on the same courses and asked "*How do I get started?*" The answer was to begin getting clients through referrals from the friends and family I'd been practising on.

It's taken me a long time to build a client base, mainly through referrals, but now my home office is really needed and I'm planning to move it to a larger room or maybe even rent rooms in a local business centre.

Trawling the yellow pages directory, I discovered that there were local clinics providing similar therapies, so I contacted them and now run sessions as part of their programme. The office at home keeps track of work at the clinic, and also my private practice that's beginning to build.

Pat

ARTIST / DESIGNER STRUGGLING

When I left college two years ago to set up as an artist and designer, I didn't realise that running myself as a business was critical for my success.

I think there might have been some input in my final year that being a great designer wasn't going to be enough, but I may have missed that course, as I was concentrating on creating my portfolio. I now realise that what you do as a professional is only half the story – operating as a business is the critical other part.

I didn't have an office to begin with, but eventually found a fellow former student who also realised that our options were either to get a job or become freelance, and that to work independently we needed an office and skills such as marketing, which were completely new to us. "*Me, doing something as ordinary as marketing? Certainly not, I'm an artist!*"

We soon got over that nonsense and created an office of sorts in her parents' spare room, with equipment supplied and financed jointly by the two sets of parents. The office is pretty basic, but enough to serve our current needs and we are now struggling to learn the business skills we need.

However, when we begin to build a client base, we'll need to know more about running an office, databases and other mysterious business activities. At the moment, we're learning about marketing, as we've discovered that being superb artist and designer is not enough.

These days, artists from whatever discipline (musician, writer, artist or performer) need to be able to set themselves up as a business with an office. If they don't, they may create but will be unseen, as the world needs to know about them, and this will only happen by being successful as a business, as well as being a great performer.

Natalie

Organise your home office

Resources

GENERAL ORGANISING BOOKS

Allen, David: *Getting Things Done*, Viking Penguin, 2001. www.davidco.com

Aslett, Don: *Freedom from Clutter*, Exley Publications Ltd, 1992.

Beattie, Melodie: *Co-dependent No More: How to Stop Controlling Others and Start Caring for Yourself.* Harper/Hazelden, 1987.

Caunt, John: *Organise Yourself.* Kogan Page, 2006.

Davidson, J: *The 60 Second Organizer*, Adams Media, 2008.

Eisenberg, Ronni: *Organise Your Office.* Hyperion, 1994.

Paul, Marilyn: *Why am I so Disorganised? Sort Out Your Stuff*. Piatkus Books Ltd, 2005.

Redway, Kathryn: *Beat the Bumph!* Nicholas Brealey, 1995.

Ricco, Monica: *Organize Your Office in No Time.* Que Publishing, 2006.

Richardson, Cheryl: *Take Time For Your Life.* Broadway Books, 1999. www.cherylrichardson.com

Walter, Dawna: *The Great Office Detox.* Penguin / Michael Joseph, 2007.

Young, Pam; Jones, Peggy: *Sidetracked Home Executives.* Warner Books, 2001. www.shesintouch.com

Young, Pam; Jones, Peggy: *Get Your Act Together.* Harper Perrenial, 1993.

ORGANISING YOUR BUSINESS

Kegan, Robert; Lahey, Lisa: *How the Way We Talk Can Change the Way We Work.* Jossey-Bass, 2001.

Cohen, Sam and team: *Learning as Leadership.* www.learnaslead.com

Paul, Marilyn: *Moving From Blame to Accountability.* The Systems Thinker, 1997.

MANAGING YOUR TIME

Morgenstern, Julie: *Time Management from the Inside Out.* Henry Holt, 2000.

Rechtschaffen, Stephan: *TimeShifting*. Doubleday, 1996.

ONLINE ORGANISATION SUPPORT GROUPS

www.flylady.net
http://www.cherylrichardson.com/forums/

PROFESSIONAL ORGANISERS

APDO - The Association of Professional Declutterers and Organisers UK. www.apdo-uk.co.uk

Organise Your World
www.organizeyourworld.com

INDEX

achievement, 28, 57, 63, 70, 71, 74, 128, 129, 131, See SMART
achieving. *See* achievement
action, 31, 36, 39, 55, 63, 65, 70, 81, 103, 104, 110
   delayed, 41
   future, 126–30
   points, 35, 140
action list. *See* lists
aggressive, 67, 74
Amy's story, 31, See also habits
archiving, 120–22
artists, 42, 142–45
assertive, 67, 74

back-up, 115, 119, 121–23
behaviour, 31, 44, 62, 74, *See also* habits
beliefs, 47, 61, 81
bookcases. *See* furniture
books, 34, 40, 87, 103
   organisation, 147, 148
   time management, 148
bumph, 109, 147

calm, 42, 131
chaos, 19, 22, 42, 55, 60, 81
charity, 11, 61, 72
checklists. See lists
clear vision, 130–31, 130–31
clutter, 40, 41, 81, 87–88, 94, 115
colleagues, 13, 37, 42, 79, 92, 97, 98
commitment, 11, 23, 31, 41, 55, 62
concentration, 35, 109
conscious self, 49
cupboards. *See* furniture

day book, 36
deadlines, 34, 45–46, 55, 68, 75, 92–95, 104
   original meaning, 75
decision
   clarification, 77
   identifying options, 77
decision-making
   improved, 77–78
   slow, 40
delegation, 35, 97–99
designers, 42, 142–45
desktop
   bombsite, 36
diary, 36, 45, 94
disorganisation, 19, 22, 26–37, 48, 53, 60, 62, 81
disorganised. *See* disorganisation
distract, 12, 35, 46, 61, 87, 109
dividers, 22
documents, 21–23, 34, 35, 36, 72, 101–7, 96, 115, 118
Donna's story, 32

editing, 105–6
educational, 19
electronic filing, 120–22
electronic tracking, 119
emails, 11, 19, 33, 34, 39, 66, 91, 94, 130, 140, 141
excuses, 46, 48, *See* procrastination
external contacts, 37

family, 13, 15, 71, 89, 135, 142, 143
files, 15, 35, 36, 41, 86, 87, 115, 117, 138, See filing
filing, 13, 36, 45, 77, 107, 96, 130, 131
   electronic, 120–22

149

filing cabinet. *See* furniture
flexi-time, 11
folders. *See* files
freelance, 11, 144
furniture, 14, 36, 42, 74, 87, 88, 92, 115, 119
future action. See plan

goals, 19, 43, 78, 65, 71, 73–76, 86, 104, 111, 120, 126–30

habits, 31–32, 79, 127, 130
    bad habits, 47–48
    building new habits, 77
    effective working, 76–77
    reinforcement, 77
home-based workers, 11

impatience, 39–40
information, 40, 45, 77, 81, 105, 136, 137, *See* documents, emails
    management, 96
interruptions, 34, 46, 61, 90–91, 96
IT specialists, 138

jobsharers, 11
journals, 33, 103, *See* magazines

kitchen, 20, 42, 90, 92, 136

letter, 30, 33, 34
lists, 71–72, 73–76, 92–95, 95–96, 101, 118, 128, 129

magazines, 33
mail, 33, *See* emails, post
managing director, 15
managing your time. *See* time
measurable. *See* SMART
meetings, 35, 45, 70, 89, 99, 140
memo, 34, 105, *See* report
memory, 34, 114
multi-tasking, 39–40, 136

musicians, 42, 142–45

neat, 47, See order

objectives, 31, 63, 67, 70, 74, *See* goals
office admin, 45
office management, 20, 45
office problems, 37, 46, 73, 83
office services, 12, 97
office specialists. *See* specialists
order, 22, 42–43, 47, 48, 131, 138
organised, 26–37
organising cycle, 47
organising needs, 37
organising personality, 33
organising tools, 43

paperless office, 139–41
papers, 36, 40, 87, *See* documents
part-time workers, 11, 138
perseverance, 31
personal life, 13, 41, 62
personal relations, 40
personality
    organising. *See* organising personality
    work style. *See* work style personality
phone, 34, 76, 91, 92, 94, 96, 135, 136, 139, 141
physical boundaries, 13
plan, 31, 63, 70, 104, 126–30, *See* planning
planning, 14, 23, 36, 41, 68, 67–71, *See* plan
ponderer, 40
post, 12, 33
post-it notes. See documents
priorities, 19, 27, 65, 127, 128, 136
procedures, 39, 139
process, 47

procrastination, 19, 34, 41, 43, 45–46, 68, 92–95, 104
productive, 43, 47
professional, 19
professional organisers, 148

quality time, 135, 138
questionnaire, 32–37

reading, 34, 99–103, 96
reinforcement. *See* habits
report, 15, 34, 39
reputation, 41, 62, 93
resources, 146–48
results oriented. *See* SMART

satisfaction, 27
secretary, 15
self-assessment, 28–44
sensitive worker, 42–43
shredder, 36
slow down, 40
SMART, 73–76
snapshots of office life, 134–45
specialists, 45, 138
specific. *See* SMART
speed demon, 39–40
storage furniture. *See* furniture
stress, 42, 43, 67, 81
students, 11
success, 27, 41, 54, 63, 64, 74, 76, 93, 140, 144
support, 13, 49, 61, 63, 62–64, 95, 98, 137, 148

targets. *See* goals
tasks, 95–96
technical support, 45
therapist, 145
time, 11, 12, 13, 31, 35, 36, 39, 44–50, 55, 62, 66, 76, 78, 81, 104, 127, 135, 148
  management, 68–69, 73–76, 90–99
time related. *See* SMART
timid, 67, 74
To Do list. See lists
typing, 45, 71, 77, 140

unconscious self, 49
unwanted material, 36

vision, 31, 127
visual worker, 41–42
voicemail, 91, 92
voluntary, 11

weaknesses, 32–37
work style personality, 29, 37–44
workbook, 21–23, 68, 102, 114, 128
workers, 11
working practice, 40
working practices, 44
workspace, 13, 14, 36, 54, 74, 76
writing, 103–5

FINALLY...

YOUR HOME OFFICE IS YOUR BEST SUPPORT FOR WHATEVER YOU WANT TO ACHIEVE THERE, SO...

MAKE THE MOST OF IT !

Now you know how to work effectively, take full advantage of the new opportunities that you have created for yourself - enjoy your new uncluttered life.

www.getlifeorganised.com

HERE'S TO
GOOD ORGANISING !

About the author

Dr Sandy Clyne has a PhD in organisation psychology from Manchester University. Most of her professional life has focused on management development within organisations and businesses.

Following an initial fascination with the question:

"What makes the difference between organisations SUCCEEDING and FAILING?"

Sandy has explored this question throughout her career, working in Business Schools, training and development departments, in both the private and public sector.

Most recently, as an advisor to small businesses, she became aware of the problems people have in setting up their office at home. This led to this book on organising your home office.

Dr Sandy Clyne

Printed in Great
Britain
by Amazon